MANAGING GRIEF
WISELY

MANAGING GRIEF
WISELY

STANLEY P. CORNILS

BAKER BOOK HOUSE
Grand Rapids, Michigan

ISBN: 0-8010-2323-8

First printing, February 1967
Second printing, September 1967
Third printing, June 1971
Fourth printing, September 1974

PHOTOLITHOPRINTED BY CUSHING - MALLOY, INC.
ANN ARBOR, MICHIGAN, UNITED STATES OF AMERICA
1977

INTRODUCTION

In this booklet we shall be thinking primarily of grief as a result of the loss of a loved one by death. As we discuss what we believe to be the better ways of handling the problem, we must bear in mind that the same techniques we mention here would be applicable to a greater or lesser degree in any situation of separation.

The purpose of this booklet is to help you to understand what is happening to you, why you feel the way you do, and why you sometimes might be tempted to believe that you are losing your mind. Here we shall attempt to define the meaning and purpose of grief — one's reactions to it — and the most therapeutic methods of handling it.

If you are in the first and acute stage of grief at the time you are introduced to this booklet, you will, no doubt, feel little interest in reading anything because your power of concentration is greatly lessened. However, may we suggest that you scan the table of contents and then begin reading at any point that seems to speak to your need.

Stanley P. Cornils

First Baptist Church
Vallejo, California

CONTENTS

 WE MUST FACE IT

Eventually sorrow finds its way into the lives of most of us. It is unlikely that we can go through life without somewhere, sometime, passing through an experience of grief. Frequently grief is associated with the loss of a loved one in death, but it is not necessarily limited to bereavement. Grief may come as a result of many other circumstances: it may come when a member of the family goes into the armed forces or away to school; it may be the result of separation during times of war; or it may come to a father or mother when a child goes out into the world to make his own way. Irrespective of its cause — grief is an emotional pain that everyone must face.

Death rides beside us every day. It is a universal experience. In our world, everything that lives will ultimately die; hence, we should be mindful of the possibility of death and include it in our philosophy of life. To face reality is a part of wisdom. It is said, that Louis XV of France decreed that the word "death" should never be spoken in his presence, and that everything that might remind him of it be removed from his sight. Refusal to face up to a problem does not nullify the problem nor does it make it go away.

Bereavement is not a unique phenomenon; it comes to all of us. If we have recently lost a loved one, the experience is new only to us. In the midst of our feelings of bewilderment and loss, we might find it helpful to remember that since time began millions have lived through the experience victoriously.

Just as a physician follows well-defined and accepted techniques in restoring vital organs to wholeness and health, we all need to follow some basic rules in the control and management of grief. Now is the time to stop to take inventory of what is going on inside us. Unfortunately, death and grief may embarrass some of us who have had so little experience with it that we neither understand it nor know how to respond to it. Perhaps, because we have had so little experience with death, we have no criteria for knowing whether or not our responses are natural and normal. Under most circumstances a physician can chart the course of convalescence and recovery following surgery. He tells us that the first few days following surgery we will be very aware of pain and may care very little whether "school keeps" or not. However, he assures us that after a week or ten days we shall be able to return home and that after a few more weeks we can return to work, and ultimately be completely well. The physician's insight encourages us to bear the discomfort an hour at a time as we progress toward complete recovery. Through the physician's help, we understand what is happening to us — we come to know what is normal and are better able to bear up under the temporary discomfort.

It is natural for us to avoid pain; nevertheless, there are many painful experiences that may come to us in the course of our life-time. We may not be able to prevent their coming, but as creative personalities, we have it within our power to determine what these experiences will do to us and how we will cope with them when they do come. We must decide how we will interpret them. Will we look upon the incident as a period of a sentence — a sign of termination that brings life to an abrupt halt? Will we regard death as a semicolon which indicates a change in direction, or will we look upon it as a colon which precedes an explanation or indicates a pause? The choice of interpretation rests with us and with us alone! We need an emotional strategy that will help us manage bereavement positively rather than negatively. The better part of wisdom in dealing with grief would be to *admit to its presence* — accept it as a reality and then set about to discover the proper technique for dealing with it.

Students of psychology have demonstrated that there are resources within us and available to us that enable us to recover from such traumatic experiences as bereavement. Most grief reactions eventually diminish in severity of and by themselves. That lessening of grief does not mean that we will ever get to the point where the sense of bereavement will cease to be; the feeling of loss will always be with us. But it is also true that there are forces and powers within us that enable us to meet and act upon the conflicts of life in a creative manner.

Not what happens to us, but how we deal with situations will determine the end result. If life throws a dagger at us, there are two ways of catching it: either by the blade or by the handle. When the world gave Jesus a cross, He accepted the worst thing that could ever happen to a man and transformed it into the greatest victory that has occurred in the world. He did not just bear the cross; He used it! And in so doing He made it a symbol of glory and honor and victory with which we decorate our heroes. Grief does not have to run like a prairie fire out of control — it can and ought to be intelligently managed.

The beauty and opalescence of the pearl presents an object lesson in the proper handling of a difficulty. A cultured pearl is formed by removing a young oyster from the sea and placing within its shell a tiny grain of sand or small pebble. The oyster is then returned to the ocean floor. No one can doubt that the oyster is irritated by this foreign substance within its body, but because it is powerless to get rid of it, it does something else. Hour by hour, day by day, and year by year, the oyster envelops the foreign body with an iridescent film which gradually becomes as hard as stone. This is how a pearl comes into being. Years later the oyster is retrieved and the beautiful pearl is harvested.

The experiences of life come to all of us, much as raw material goes into a factory, and the finished product that comes out on the loading dock is the result of the skill and effort of the craftsmen within the factory. We may see the same principle at work as we watch two small children on the floor playing with similar sets of blocks. One may construct something of childish beauty or interesting intricacy, while the other may fashion something crude or clumsy, or maybe nothing at all. Like the workers in the factory and the children playing on the floor — we largely determine the end result.

This principle might best be illustrated by the Oriental story of Yussef and Ahmed, two young men who day after day sat weaving at their looms. Each morning they were given a supply of yarn for the day, brilliantly colored to represent the galaxy of human emotions. There were many colors among the skeins of yarn. One day there was delivered to both of them a large heap of the black yarn of Sorrow. Yussef was discouraged by such a stark color and he wove the yarn into his pattern in harsh patches. On the other hand, Ahmed used his allotment of black yarn differently and wove it into his design with understanding Sympathy. There were golden threads of Happiness, purple threads of Pain, and blue threads of Discouragement. Yussef did not bother to use many of them. The colors he did choose he shot with bitterness into his pattern. With bold artistry Ahmed skillfully blended his allotment of precious threads with care and tenderness into the pattern as he wove. When the Master came to inspect their tapestries, Yussef growled that he had not been given the proper yarn; his tapestry was mediocre — almost worthless. But when the Master examined Ahmed's work, he found it a masterpiece of the weaver's art. Ahmed had mingled light with shadow. Then the Master gently said to the two craftsmen, "Both of you had the same materials, and you used them as you wished. It is not what comes to your life that determines the pattern, but the use you make of it."

If we react to sorrow in a positive and creative way, it may bring a whole new dimension to our lives. A diamond has many facets, and so has a life. Eyes that have never known tears may lack genuine tenderness. The heart that has never been torn by anguish from the loss of a loved one has never sounded its own depths. Only as grief enters into and becomes blended with other elements of our personalities can we emerge as full and mature persons. We grow strong through storm and conflict. Someone has suggested that we never "are"; we are always "becoming." We are the unfinished masters of an unfinished world. After the experience of mourning has run its course, there will be wounds that still ache; there will be losses still hard to bear; but no matter how we may feel about the sorrow itself, most of us would be unwilling to surrender what it has brought and taught us, and we would be reluctant to go back to being the kind of persons we were before the sorrow came to us. The softening, hallowing touch of grief leaves its indelible mark upon our personalities.

# GRIEF IS AN EMOTION

Grief is a many-faceted complex of emotions. It involves our deepest feelings, and — as with any other emotion that we may experience — we must decide how we will meet and manage it. We may deny it; we may delay it; we may repress it; or we may accept it and express it as best we can.

What really happens when we react properly to an emotion? How do we control it positively? Every emotion calls for action: the emotion of anger often results in a desire to retaliate; the emotion of love needs the opportunity to express itself; the emotion of fear may cause us to run. Fortunately, most of our emotional episodes provide us with opportunities for action and for understanding the source and cause of the emotion. The emotion of grief, however, is not always so simple to deal with because we can do nothing about the loss which brought it on, namely, the death of a loved one. Death is one messenger to whom we cannot talk back.

Emotions are very real, and we must deal with them realistically. As with any other emotion, we may force grief out of our consciousness through denial or delay. We may not admit to the loss of a loved one by refusing to think of his death. We may even dispose of the personal effects of our beloved or discard all pictures and mementos of the life and experiences shared with the deceased in an effort to begin a new mode of life that will help us to become successful in forgetting.

However, the denial of expression to emotion does not necessarily destroy or dissipate it. We may merely push it further into the subconscious mind to be confined much like the steam in a pressure cooker. There, in the subconscious, the emotion may stay until its pressure becomes so strong that it will escape in some disguised form, such as nervous exhaustion or some other debility. Psychological and medical research indicates that various types of neuroses and even physical distress can be traced to an experience of bereavement in which grief was repressed and mishandled. "Keeping your chin up" does not really solve anything finally. In trying to follow such a course we may be fooled into a false sense of maturity that we do not actually possess. Instead of manifesting a strong expression of faith, we are trying to develop a false sense of peace by short-circuiting our emotional processes.

THE WORK OF MOURNING

Grief is normally resolved by mourning, a process generally referred to as "grief work" or "the work of mourning." To do this work successfully we who are bereaved work our way mentally, emotionally, and even physically through the various stages of grief. We shall speak of these stages in the pages following as (1) acceptance, (2) expression, (3) emancipation and (4) readjustment. The challenge we face is that of learning to accept the reality of the separation and to give up, little by little, our emotional dependence on the object of our grief, the one who no longer can share life with us. Only after this has been completed will our lives resume a normal and meaningful pattern. It is only when we try to skip "the work of mourning" that we get into trouble.

"Grief work" is hard work; it is painful and involves suffering. But much like the pain of childbirth, it is a pain with a purpose: it brings forth something. Although the experience may be very distressing, the work of normal mourning is helpful rather than injurious to the bereaved. At times the process may become so very difficult that we are tempted to retreat from reality. Mourning also involves tension: tension resulting from the physical absence and the very real memories of the presence of the departed. True, the person has left us physically, but he has not gone from our emotions. We are torn between a natural longing for our loved one and a recognition of the fact that he is no longer present as a physical reality.

Our attachment to our loved one will lessen gradually but not effortlessly. Only as we succeed in doing our "grief work" will we again become free and uninhibited. Unless we do the work of mourning properly, we will remain out of touch with reality and be held in bondage to the lost loved one, and we will be thwarted in our efforts to progress through and beyond the experience.

There is no miraculous way to avoid the pain resulting from a surgical operation or the healing of a broken bone. Neither can we look for or expect a miraculous healing of our grief. We can ill afford to become impatient with the slow pathway of healing that leads from sorrow to renewed serenity. We are foolish to attempt prematurely to telescope these successive stages of recuperation and hope for a miraculous cure. We will suffer pain, poignant grief, empty days, resistance to consolation, and disinterestedness in life in general.

However, if we are courageous and resolute we will again be able to live as our loved one would have wished us to live and face life bravely and undismayed instead of being lonely, embittered, and made hollow by self-pity. In our present bewilderment it might be difficult to realize that this could ever happen to us or that life could ever again be meaningful for us. But let us look around us and count our many acquaintances who have triumphed over sorrow. Their victories can also be ours, for it is possible to restore the abnormal to the normal through the healing process involved in doing our grief work.

THE MANIFESTATIONS
OF GRIEF

Just as there is a common pattern of symptoms and reactions peculiar to a medical disease, so there is, also, a pattern of symptoms and reactions experienced by most people in acute grief. These reactions do not necessarily occur immediately following the loss of a loved one. Sometimes they are repressed or delayed; sometimes they are exaggerated; sometimes they are apparently absent.

When anything is as common as death, we assume that the reaction to it will be normal, and in most instances it is. When the blunt fact of bereavement hits, and the announcement is made that death has come, most of us are benumbed and bewildered. This numbing effect is the result of our emotional inability to accept the fact of death in a realistic way. Some of us may become hysterical and suffer emotional and even physical paralysis. We are apt to lose our equilibrium and our traditional patterns of conduct. The world has become dead to us — a dreary wasteland with only grief, loneliness, and despair to possess our souls. The situation does not seem real. We may feel that "this cannot be happening to us — this is all a dream, and soon we will awaken to find that it is not real." Because weeping is our first response to pain, tears may be our first reaction to the loss of our loved one. We may weep prolongedly and hysterically.

These initial reactions may last from twenty minutes to several hours; they should be regarded as surface in nature for they seem to have little bearing on our prospect for future adjustment.

Our grief will either completely control and manage us, or we will learn to control and manage it. Needless to say, many of us never conquer grief — instead we are conquered by it. If we allow it, grief can and will destroy us. What it does to us will be determined by how we respond to it. Someone has suggested that grief is like a bewitched pogo-stick: it will make us jump in some direction, but which way we know not unless we have had previous experience in using it. The child who has spent many hours and experienced many bruises in learning to ride the pogo-stick ultimately can make it take him where he wants to go. The spectre of our grief can be transfigured; our sorrow can become a sacrament; and we can learn to be victorious over our grief if only we will learn how to control it intelligently.

Because grief is such a painful experience, our natural tendency is to run from it and resort to anything that will help us bypass the pain for the time being. Not infrequently a physician will prescribe sedatives to help us through the first stages of our grief experience, and such medication may prove to be a real help in our time of great need, but sedatives should be used sparingly and only in situations where there is real mental abnormality. The normal reaction to loss should run its course and not be suppressed. More often than not, sedation only delays the reaction and the longer "the work of mourning" is delayed, the more difficult it will be to control grief effectively. If we try to circumvent the emotional stress of grief, we may succeed only in delaying the cure. *The work of mourning should not be postponed.*

Following the initial onset of grief, waves of acute distress may overcome us when we are reminded of the deceased. The throat tightens; we experience a choking sensation and a shortness of breath; we may lack power; we climb a flight of stairs or walk to the corner and feel exhausted; our every activity becomes an effort; we feel a weight on our chest; we may gulp in long, sobbing sighs as though fighting for air; our appetites vanish; our saliva ceases to flow; our food tastes like sawdust; our bowel and kidney actions may become irregular. Nothing has meaning; everyone seems far away; nothing seems real. The lights of the heavens seem to have gone out and we feel we are left in desolation and darkness. When someone demonstrates kindness, sympathy, or recalls a sacred memory, we become overwhelmed by our sorrow.

There are still other possible reactions: we may have a feeling of emptiness or of living in a dream; we may become hostile; we may behave in a stiff and formal manner; we may react toward other people with irritation and even anger; we may become obsessed with the mental image of the deceased; we may exhibit complete disinterestedness in our environment; we may deviate from our normal pattern of conduct; we may manifest a disorganized and undependable attitude; we may feel that we are losing our mind; we may want to talk incessantly about the lost one; we may have a feeling of restlessness as we repeat motions without zest or meaning.

We have little or no capacity to initiate or organize activity; we procrastinate; we may sometimes imitate traits and mannerisms of the deceased, especially those dominant during the last illness; we may imitate a gait or be absorbed by an interest in the things the deceased was interested in; we may feel an emotional separation from other people and a resentment toward everyone whose life has been undisturbed.

To any of us who are novices to grief, it may seem that such a long list of symptoms and complications is unrealistic. We must remember, however, that in losing our loved one a part of our larger self has been amputated; life's pattern has been upset; our focus on life has become blurred, and until we acquire a new focus, we must accept the fact that our scheme of life may be disorganized.

Almost everyone of us who loses a loved one should expect these reactions. They are all within the range of normalcy. If we understand them and do our "grief work" courageously, we will express rather than repress our emotions by readjusting our attitudes and forming new relationships. In this way we may discover a true and therapeutic strategy for dealing with our grief. This mental detour does not mean that there will come a day when we will no longer feel our loss, but when we have succeeded in placing limits on our own selfish interests, we shall have gone a long way toward mastering our grief.

ACCEPTANCE

Acceptance is the first link we must forge in the experience of bereavement if we are to deal with it successfully. Although the terminal illness of our loved one may have been lengthy and taxing and death may have been expected for weeks or even months, we are never ready for it when it does come.

Most of us come to realize quite early in our experience of living that we will be spending much of our lives becoming accustomed to things we had not anticipated. Bereavement is one of these things. When the telegraph messenger comes to our door with a message, what do we do? Shut the door in his face, refuse to accept the message, or try to run away? Wisdom suggests that we accept the message, because no matter what action we take, we cannot change the content of the message he brings. In real life we would accept the message and act accordingly. So must we accept death, admit to it, and face it as a reality; for if we fail to accept death realistically, we will also fail in handling it intelligently and creatively.

It is not being heroic to continue as though nothing has happened, because something *has* happened. We feel we have lost a vital part of ourselves. Trying to escape from reality is not being heroic. We cannot settle anything without settling it aright, and the problem of grief cannot be dealt with correctly and creatively until we have faced it and accepted it. When we dodge or bypass or run away from grief, we find only a temporary refuge, but sooner or later grief will track us down and we will have to deal with it.

Psychology today offers much evidence to show that personality grows by confronting the conflicts of life positively and constructively rather than by circumventing them. We do not become wholesome, creative individuals by walling ourselves off from our conflicts or by opening gates for a hasty retreat. It is far more therapeutic for us to recognize, face, and conquer the conflicting issues of life. In dealing properly with these conflicts, we discover all the available resources that can contribute to our further growth.

Our social system provides us with many ways of masking the stark reality of death. We refer to our dead loved ones as having "passed away," as "being asleep," or as "having departed." It would be better for us if we were not so afraid of the word "death." Calling it some other name does not solve our problem, nor does such a reference help us to believe "there is no death." The poet's words just quoted are true because they imply life everlasting. Death does not mean extinction. However, physical death is very real.

We would not decry the magnificent artistry of the mortician and the comforting appointments of the modern funeral home. Funeral directors and their surroundings have done much to lessen the shock of bereavement; but when we regard these as means of denying the fact of physical death, we are in need of help. Our attempts to disguise the reality of death reflect a desire to treat death as unreal, as if we could ease the pain of our loss by denying its reality. This dilemma creates a serious conflict within us who know the reality of our loss more keenly than anyone else could ever know it, and yet all around us so much is being done to deny or disguise it. We cannot do anything constructive about trouble by refusing to accept it or by running away from it. In trying to elude the reality of death, we only harbor and nourish a mood that may bring us into greater difficulty unless we find a way to rise above it.

There is an old story of an oak tree and a reed which grew close to each other on the side of a hill. One day the wind came with hurricane force, threatening to destroy them both. The oak stiffened its branches and prepared to fight, but the reed only quivered in terror. After the storm had passed, the oak lay uprooted on its side while the reed, uninjured, soon stood as straight and tall as ever. When the dying oak asked the reed what made the difference, the reed replied: "I bent with the wind; I accepted it."

EXPRESSION OR SUPPRESSION

One of the laws governing human nature holds, in effect, that an emotion, once touched off, ushers in a chain of events within the body which in some way or another must be externalized by some sort of action if the cycle is to be complete. This action — chemical, skeleto-muscular, neural, or mental — will automatically discharge the energy produced by the emotion. The emotional chain is never completed until the appropriate act or its substitute has been performed. For most of us, our first reaction to the death of a loved one gives rise to a feeling of numbness, and even disbelief. But what is to be regarded as normal beyond this point?

We can conclude from studies made in this field that there is only one remedy for grief, and that is to grieve. We should not be ashamed to grieve. We should give vent to grief as we feel it. The ancient Jews had a custom that allowed for a week of mourning, during which the bereaved and his friends were allowed to talk about the deceased and his virtues. This custom was a wise and a healthful one, for there is a close relation between the healing of physical wounds and the healing of emotional wounds. If we are injured, our blood flows freely to cleanse the wound and then to heal it. So it is with our grief. If we allow it to flow freely and thereby purge itself, our emotional wound will heal. But if we distort, conceal, or deny our normal feelings, we provide fertile grounds for a breakdown. We should allow a bleeding heart a clear leeway for its expression of grief. Instead of distracting our attention from our bereavement (a procedure that should come much later in the healing process), we should speak of our loss, talk of our sorrow, and eulogize the beauty and virtues of our departed one.

There are those who object to a display of grief because they fear that such expression may lead to a nervous collapse. Actually, the opposite is true. Normally, we do not come apart at the seams emotionally as a result of expression of nervous or emotional reaction; more often than not a nervous breakdown results from the repression of emotions. The more we express our grief, the better will be our emotional health in the long run. In essence, we get well by suffering.

Many of us who suppress grief may only deceive ourselves and others into thinking that we are thereby overcoming it. We seldom overcome grief so easily for grief does not dissolve by suppression. It merely slips underground where it may produce a psychotic illness or cause subtle and damaging changes to our personalities. When we repress any negative emotion (including grief), the emotion is not necessarily dispelled; it may only be building up to volcanic proportions. When the eruption finally does come, the consequences can be more serious than if we had faced and accommodated rather than repressed our original feelings. Feelings walled up within ourselves mean trouble ahead.

 # TEARS AND TALK

Tears are important in the nurturing of the spirit, but do we really understand the function and meaning of them? God gave us tears for a purpose. There are few things as comforting and soothing as the consoling effect of quiet tears; for tears have the power to dissolve the many tensions inherent in our experiences with sorrow. Tears, warm and wet, are soothing and can do much to help wash away the irritants of our lives.

We should not be ashamed of legitimate tears or feel guilty about shedding them. We may discover that we can see farther through a tear than through a telescope. Weeping can be appropriate, noble, and majestic. Our tears can be crystallized into lenses through which we can better see God's purpose for us and our loved one. God washes our eyes with tears so that we may see the otherwise invisible land where tears shall be no more.

Talking about our sorrow also helps release tension and dissolve the pain of the grief experience. It is true that each time we talk about a painful experience, our pain is eased just a little more. It is by speaking to others of our loss and sorrow that we learn to bear pain. Memories of our loved one may continue to come back to us, but their power to hurt will have been dissipated.

Talking also has a therapeutic value. First, it is cathartic. When we verbalize, we help release the pent-up tensions resulting from grief. An angry man yells; a terrified woman screams; and a bereaved person sheds tears and talks. Through verbalization our feelings of loss, loneliness, guilt, anger, and hostility toward the departed are brought to the surface of our consciousness where we can deal with them.

In the second place, talking provides us with insight, which enables us to see more clearly our real feelings and problems. We should not be afraid of verbalizing our feelings of anger and hostility toward our loved ones because we should recognize that they too possessed the weaknesses and failings of mankind. Only after we have achieved this insight will we discover that new feelings and reactions will be forthcoming.

In the third place, the talking process establishes a wholesome relationship with the persons in whom we confide. In a very real sense, they help us bear our sorrow by knowing our feelings about it.

A few words of caution should be spoken at this point concerning the expression of our grief. First of all, when the death of a loved one interrupts our normal pattern of life, we may try to cope with our loss by rationalizing. We may attempt to exercise extreme self-control, acting as though nothing had happened. We may seek new interests in life and exhibit great bursts of energy and enthusiasm as we become overly busy in our efforts to avoid loneliness and memories. Some of us may seek to "cover up" by embarking on some kind of a binge, forgetting that we cannot drink, smoke, work, play, or eat our way out of grief nor find the solution to any of our problems by carrying on any activity solely for escape.

Our second word of caution has to do with a tendency and temptation to syndicate our sorrows.

They should not be shared with everyone we meet. We recall the story of a boy who had a sore thumb and who told everyone he met about his hurt as he painfully unwound the bandage before the eyes of all who would listen to his tale of woe. His sore thumb not only dominated his horizon but also the horizons of all who knew him. Every time they thought of him they remembered his sore thumb. So with us; how much better it would be for us and our friends, if when they think of us, they would not think of us as being obsessed by sorrow, but as courageously mastering our sorrow!

In the third place we must be careful that the social pressures of our culture do not prohibit us from doing the kind of mourning that will have a therapeutic effect. Our culture has a rather highly developed pattern which our reactions of grief should follow. There are certain established duties required of us who are mourners. We curtail and restrict our social activities and dress somberly in a mode symbolic of the feelings a bereaved person should have. We as mourners may thereby find ourselves between the two horns of a dilemma. On the one hand, we may feel the necessity for the "proper amount of tears" to demonstrate and prove our affection for the departed; and on the other hand, we may try to "bear up wonderfully." Despite the fact that during the past few generations our culture has made much progress in a better direction, it is still necessary for us to remember that by trying to satisfy the social demands for a particular type of mourning (which is usually superficial and has little regard for our true feelings) we may also be substituting this type of surface mourning for the deeper experience of grieving which is really necessary and we may thereby fail to find real and permanent healing. The proper response to our loss will probably be the one that comes most naturally.

The final word of warning has to do with an excessive display of grief. There is a thought-provoking passage in Rabbinic wisdom that says: "It is impossible not to mourn, but to mourn excessively is forbidden." Excessive grief is seldom a genuine way of showing devotion to our departed loved one. Would it please our loved one to see us so completely given over to sorrow that we are beside ourselves to the point where no one can do anything with us or for us? Excessive grief more often than not brings in its wake deterioration of the personality, upset digestion, malfunctioning of the bodily organs, and a general impairment of health.

In the Jewish Talmud there is a story of a man who had a little girl, his only daughter, who became sick and died. His heart was broken. Despite all the efforts of his friends to comfort him and help him realize that life does go on, he refused to be comforted.

One night he dreamed that he was in heaven and saw little girls in a pageant. Each girl carried a lighted candle. The candle carried by his own daughter was unlit. As he took her in his arms and caressed her he asked, "Why is your candle not lit?" She answered, "Sometimes it does light, but your tears always put it out."

It is natural for us to be disturbed, heartbroken and concerned when a loved one is taken from us. But to despair over-much and to be unwilling to recognize God and the eternal life he gives us is both unwise and unhealthy. The sun always rises to shine through the clouds after the darkest night, but constant tears and lamenting will prevent us from seeing the light.

 EMANCIPATION

The third step in doing our grief work involves learning how to free ourselves from the bondage of the physical existence and coexistence with the loved one. This means that we must go over and over the memories of our former associations with the loved one until we are sufficiently emancipated and free to go on and assume new relationships. Unless we do this, we will make little progress and we will be out of vital touch with reality.

Because bereavement is difficult to accept, we attempt to retreat to a magic world of memories dominated by our loved one. We may set an extra place at the table for the deceased, as though he were to be present, converse with him at the graveside, or summon his spirit for advice. These are touching evidences of our devotion, but such practices are inadequate substitutes for "grief work" and may even handicap us in performing our responsibilities to the living and can delay our readjustment to life and possibly threaten our mental and physical health. As long as we try to keep our sorrow alive artificially, it will continue. As long as we use a trick — and we know it is a trick — we are in control of the situation, but when we begin to fool ourselves, the trick is controlling us, and we are in need of help.

We will achieve mental balance if we will courageously accept and live through the pangs of loneliness rather than attempt to evade them. It is true that the melody our loved one played upon the instrument of life will never be played in quite the same manner again, but this fact does not mean that we should close the keyboard and allow the instrument to gather dust. Death has disorganized our scheme of life, and it will remain that way until we develop a new perspective.

Just as mourning is necessary in performing our "grief work," so should we allow our memories to help us in our "grief work." Our well-meaning friends may avoid references to our loss because they want to help us forget, but forgetting is just what we do not want to do. In making our way through this difficult task, we should go over and over our memories of our beloved until we become emancipated and can accept new relationships within a framework from which our loved one has gone. Although this is a slow and painful process, and may even be accompanied by physical and emotional discomfort, we must face up to it and undertake it honestly and courageously. We may be surprised to discover, in time, that we can again talk about memories and meditate upon them. As we do this, our pain will grow less and we will be able to recall and adjust to additional memories.

It may help us to think of our lives as being a maze through which we and our beloved traveled together for many years. Along the pathway we left a cord to mark our journey. At many turns, we shared experiences which now have become only memories. At one turn our beloved was taken away and we were left standing alone. Are we to go on as though nothing has changed? Common sense tells us we must let our beloved go. But what do we do with all these experiences of the past? Probably the most helpful thing we can do is to pick up the cord and retrace our steps and experiences even to the time and place we began our lives together. Doing so will help us to surrender our loved one and also help us to design a new pattern for our lives, a pattern in which the loved one exists only as a memory. This does not imply that we have forsaken our attachments to our loved one, but rather that we have accepted the idea of living with a memory yet not being in bondage to it.

Mrs. Joshua Liebman, whose husband wrote *Peace of Mind,* tells of her own experience with grief following her husband's death: "To make myself realize that Joshua was really gone, and to try to function in a world without him, I began by doing alone or with Liela [their adopted daughter] the things I had formerly done with Joshua." She continues by telling of the wonderful times she and her husband had had in New York. Shortly after his death, she made her first return trip to these same places abounding in exciting and happy memories for her. She continues: "I took the bitter medicine. I gazed unseeingly into shop windows, dined without appetite at our favorite restaurants, bought tickets for theaters and movies, accepted invitations to the homes of friends. I cannot pretend that I enjoyed myself. I felt like an amputee trying to walk on artificial legs. It would be foolish for me to say that even after eight years I have entirely succeeded in conquering my grief. I still feel, as the poet Heine said, 'a toothache in my heart.' Grief's slow wisdom, I have learned, comes slowly indeed."[1] Painful is the surgery that removes so much of one's life!

So, instead of trying to forget, we should recall our relationships with the departed. We should re-live certain of our experiences in memory, think and talk freely of the deceased, and face up to the adjustments that are necessary. The process is difficult for us because it is painful. Mourning is accompanied by suffering, but by a suffering that promotes healing. Through this kind of "grief work" the relationship is truly severed: we set our loved one free and in so doing we also set our own selves free to relate to others persons and objects.

By these rational acceptances, we are transformed and can independently and resourcefully cope with the world of reality without our loved one. At first, we may be unable to tolerate the thought of the everyday occupations and activities that we associate with the departed. However, we must ponder on every object and situation, and foster the association until we can accept our loss unemotionally.

---

[1]*Woman's Home Companion,* Sept., 1956, pp. 4-6.

 ## READJUSTMENT

Mourning becomes therapeutic when we can face reality, accept our loss, and work out a new organization for living. When death terminates a happy and vital relationship, it is necessary that we find a substitute for the broken relationship. We need to discover new patterns of action and new areas of interest to compensate for the life-design interrupted by death.

These substitute patterns do not come spontaneously and effortlessly. In grief, there is no short cut to readjustment and renewed life interest. We never learn to do arithmetic by copying the results from the answer key in the book. We will know many lonely hours and empty days; often we may feel that we can never recapture an interest in human affairs.

More often than not, our grief will run its course and it will eventually decrease in severity; but if our grief is founded on a vacuum, self-pity will rush in to fill the void and a mind invaded by self-pity may become unsound. An emotional wound free of self-pity will heal normally and quickly, but if it has been infected by self-pity it may become very difficult to heal.

A very vital part of our readjustment process concerns our renewal of former relationships with other people as soon as possible and our forming and developing new interests in people and activities. The most trying days of our bereavement are not the days preceding the funeral but the first days following it. We who are bereaved evidence a tendency to build a wall around ourselves with our grief and retreat from life's stream of reality. No one individual or group of individuals can bridge the gap left by our loved ones. Friends cannot be expected to take the place of the departed in our lives, but we, as social beings, need the help that friends and the assuming of social responsibilities can give us. Despite the sudden void created by the death of our dear one, we must consider and be mindful of our devotion and responsibility to the living as well as to the dead. When sorrow overtakes us, we are tempted to drop out of affairs and retreat within ourselves in loneliness. When a rider is thrown from his horse, he must remount as soon as possible if ever he is to ride again. We, too, need to be challenged to live again. We cannot go backwards; we must move ahead. One step, then another, and then another. Activity is a very necessary part of the cure we need. By swinging into action, we can build our bridge to the future because activity is symbolic of life's forward movement. However, we should not be dismayed when we resume our social responsibilities and relationships to find ourselves somewhat unhappy and even uncomfortable in the company of those whom we should enjoy.

Every human being can build new bridges of human companionship throughout his life. This capability is not reserved for youth alone. We, as human beings, possess the ability to weave new patterns of interpersonal relationships that will make us richer, more creative, more interesting, and more dynamic individuals. Those of us who have recently undergone surgery have perhaps been surprised and even amazed when our doctor leaves orders for our nurses to get us out of bed as soon as possible, even the day following the operation. Medical scientists have discovered that the sooner an impaired organ can assume normal functioning, the more rapid will be its recovery.

Perhaps we should sound a word of caution here relative to the frequent temptation to make impulsive and radical changes in our way of living in an attempt to "get away from it all." Even though our home or apartment may be for us a storehouse of memories, we should make changes gradually, and then only after we have carefully pondered our reasons for making them. We should exercise similar caution before rushing back to our business too soon after the funeral merely to be absorbed in activity. We do not escape grief by hurrying back to anything! In so doing, we may only submerge our grief deeper within ourselves where it may long remain as an inner tension that could give rise to further complications. Any rushing back to anything may delay the contemplation that we need to help us reach the ultimate and satisfactory answers. Let us follow further the analogy of the surgical operation! The doctor also knows that unless an organ is given an opportunity to heal properly, his patient may suffer serious consequences as a result of returning to work too soon following surgery. The surgeon knows that the healing of the body takes time. It takes time, too, to recover emotional balance. Bereavement involves our emotions, and the necessity for doing our "grief work" properly is so urgent, that we should consider taking some leave time to permit us to put our emotional house in order.

 ## GUILT FEELINGS

One of the severest ordeals we as bereaved persons may experience concerns our possible feelings of guilt engendered by the death of our loved one. Many of us have guilt feelings relating to the deceased, feelings that may or may not be justified. Any feeling of guilt is disturbing. Regardless of whether our guilt feelings are justified or imagined, they are very real to us, and we must deal with them if we are to find relief.

These guilt feelings arise from our actual or fancied neglect of or wrong-doing toward the deceased. We may scourge ourselves with such thoughts as, "Why did we not take that trip while our loved one was still with us? Should we have called the doctor sooner? Why did we not call in a specialist? Why did we not get our beloved to the hospital sooner? Why had we not been more considerate and thoughtful? Why did we not spend more time with the one who has been taken from us? Why did we make as many demands of the departed? Why didn't we do this or that? If only we could do things over!" These "if only's" are the hallmarks of grief, and too often we assemble them only to fashion a veil of remorse. We need not feel responsible for another person's death. We must not assume too much. To rehearse our own set of "if only's" is like wiggling a sore tooth to make it hurt the more. It may have been too late to do anything for the departed loved one — and in all probability we did our very best. None of us can do more. Be these things as they may, we can find solace in confession and through confession learn that forgiveness awaits us.

 ## AMBIVALENCE

Contradictory emotions may also be the cause of guilt feelings which accompany grief. These guilt feelings are subtly allied with the feelings of unresolved hostility toward the departed. Nothing human is perfect. All of us experience moods of resentment and hostility even toward our most beloved persons. Our purest and noblest love may sometimes be colored by a tincture of anger. This is true because we are human — and humankind is not perfect.

Some of us may go all the way through our lives without ever admitting to ourselves or to anyone else that we have experienced moods of hatred or resentment toward our loved ones. As a result of such an attitude, many of us who have lost loved ones spend much time in our efforts to adjust to our loss by glorifying and by idealizing by thought and word the qualities of the departed. In this way, we unconsciously attempt to resolve the existing guilt feelings. We might say that such purging is our way of paying off an emotional debt.

The free expression of grief is difficult as long as we have any negative feelings toward the departed one. Both education and religion conspire to make us feel guilty of our normal aggressive impulses. Working through these feelings becomes more difficult if we are ashamed, for when we are ashamed we often attempt to conceal our feelings even from ourselves by repressing our contrition rather than by admitting it to ourselves and others. In order to keep this ambivalence from becoming obvious, we may magnify our love for the departed or protest either too much or too long and so prolong our grief. We are being much wiser when we review our unpleasant as well as pleasant relationships with the deceased. It is entirely proper for us to express our feelings in a legitimate and wholesome manner in every dimension of our lives.

ABNORMAL GRIEF

The majority of grief situations are normal. Most of us meet the crisis situations of life with enough strength of personality and momentum to get through them with a capacity we did not know we possessed. However, our grief can become morbid and abnormal when we cannot bridge the gap made by broken relationships and find comfort and solace from new ones.

Our morbid grief reactions are distortions of natural grief. There are two types of abnormal grief: the first is evidenced by a delay of reaction. Should the bereavement occur at a time when we are confronted with important tasks and the necessity for maintaining the morale of others we may exhibit little or no reaction for weeks or even much longer. We delay the grieving period, but we cannot do so indefinitely.

If we do not grieve at the time of our loss, grief will come later and perhaps at a greater cost to our whole personality. Upon the death of our beloved and for a short period afterwards, we may appear calm and composed. Later, however, we become more aware of the reaction of grief. Sometimes this delayed reaction occurs when we are near the age of the recently deceased. In most instances this delayed reaction may be attributed to our lack of experience with bereavement.

Studies made on the effect of grief indicate that a repression of emotions arising from bereavement is later apt to result in morbid reactions. Some folk become enraged and angry with the whole world without really knowing why. Others suffer a severe depression for many years following the loss of a loved one without being aware of any relation between their continued depression and the denial of their grief.

The second type of morbid reaction to bereavement that we may experience involves a change in our conduct. We may indulge in motiveless activity; we may evidence symptoms characteristic of the illness of the deceased; we may encourage and even develop psychosomatic conditions, such as rheumatoid arthritis, or asthma; we may obviously exhibit an unusual attitude toward our friends and relatives. We may feel irritable, not want to be bothered, avoid social activities, and be afraid we might alienate our friends by our lack of interest and our hypercritical attitudes. Some of us even evidence a furious hostility toward people whom we once dearly loved. Some of us, however, do succeed in concealing our hostility by becoming almost wooden and formal. Some of us forsake our former patterns of social interaction. We cannot initiate an activity, even though we are eager to be active. We become restless and cannot sleep. Finally, we may experience the ultimate in the grief reaction manifested by deep depression, severe tenseness, unwarranted insomnia, feelings of worthlessness, bitter self-accusation, and desire for chastisement. A person with these latter symptoms may be seriously in danger of self-destruction.

The appearance of these reactions should prompt us to seek the counsel and spiritual aid that will help us through our crisis, since most of these manifestations can, with proper treatment at the hands of a skilled person, be transformed into normal reactions in which the patient will find proper resolution.

 RELIGION AND GRIEF

In a large measure our religious faith will influence the way in which we will meet bereavement. Because sorrow is a spiritual pilgrimage, religion has attempted throughout the ages to give us comfort, courage, and hope for the experience. Our faith will do much to determine how the traumatic experience of bereavement will affect us. Religion deals with the meaning of life and death. Our spiritual faith has something to say about death, for religion alone provides us with the only hope for reunion with our departed loved ones.

The pages of religious literature are replete with the testimonies of those who have found a new relationship with God through their grief. Such an awakening can be ours. What we believe about the future, and how we anticipate a spiritual reunion with the departed, will determine the way we face up to sorrow and death. Those of us who have faith in God will find the mystery of death less perplexing because we believe that all of life and death are in the hands of God — this includes a belief in immortality and the conviction that we will someday be reunited with our loved ones.

Some of us for the first time come to a meaningful understanding of God through the death of a loved one. Our loss may leave an aching emptiness that will draw us to God, whom we thought we could do without. There are some who "turn to religion" to ease their grief, as though faith were some sort of soothing syrup or emotional anesthetic. This is a perversion of religion. Nor should we look upon religion as a means of safeguarding us from trouble. No matter how spiritual we may be, we share with the rest of humanity the ills common to life in our world. Just because we trust in God does not imply that we will never lose our loved ones or our health, or that we shall never be disappointed or frustrated.

Religion will not be of much value if we have never been "over the road" before. Unless we are well practiced in its techniques we may be too numb for it to be of much help. We must know how and where to go to find what we need. To be of real value in a grief experience, religion must be an integral part of our living — a way of life — not merely a blanket that we wrap around our grief. Any attempt to ride "piggy-back" on religion as we pass through our experience of sorrow will be as frustrating and unrewarding as attempting to trap quicksilver. However, religion in the life of one who has had experience in it can be a strong support in the time of sorrow; it can provide a light in the darkness of our disillusionment and despair; it can provide us with a source of power beyond human resources that will enable us to resolve a tragedy into a triumph and our sorrow into a sacrament.

Normally we express our sorrow horizontally — towards our friends, our loved ones, the world around us, and inwardly toward ourselves. It would seem that those who evidence the "faith that overcomes the world" give to their grief also a vertical expression, which has something to do with God — and they want God to have something to do with them. At a time like this we can sense the presence of God, as real and vital as breathing and nearer than hands and feet. We will never know what it really means to walk with God in the deepest sense until we have walked with Him in the dark. Any agonizing experience, if taken in stride with a loving Father's aid, will do something creative for us. The seeds of our sorrow will yield us a golden harvest of divine blessings when planted in the soil of faithful, believing hearts.

God is the source of power and provides us with strength for any situation. Most of us live in the narrow world of "self," and have not learned to cope with the difficult situations occurring in our lives. But when our world is centered in God, we come to know the "peace that passeth all understanding"; and we comprehend the meaning of the words, "Underneath are the everlasting arms." Grief does not need to be lonesome torture. We are not alone. This experience can be guided and utilized for a spiritual result. If we make use of the most wonderful of all stage directions — "Enter God" — He will come into our experience and reveal His presence in a way beyond our power to describe. We with God can work this thing out together, for He will neither leave us nor forsake us in our darkest hour. "When through the deep waters thy trials shall lie, I will be with thee." Only when we come to the end of "self," will we really come to depend upon God. And He can be depended upon!

God is always with us. "Whither shall I go from thy Spirit?" (Ps. 139:7); "God is our refuge and strength, a very present help in trouble" (Ps. 46:1); "As a father pitieth his children, so the Lord pitieth them that fear him" (Ps. 103:13); "As one whom his mother comforteth, so will I comfort you" (Isa. 66:13). Those of us who are parents are unceasingly solicitous of the comfort and well-being of our children, and especially so when a child is suffering some hurt. God, as our Father, has something for us in our grief, but He will have more for us if we came to know Him as a loving Father before the experience of grief came to us. Many of us are in accord with the Psalmist's expression of real faith when he said, "What time I am afraid, I will trust in thee" (Ps. 56:3). But Isaiah gave evidence of a more mature and creative faith in the words: "Behold, God is my salvation; *I will trust and not be afraid*" (Isa. 12:2). Isaiah's faith represents a step beyond the faith of the Psalmist.

Religion is something for us to use — not lose — during our time of bereavement. Because real and powerful sustaining comfort is one of the end products of faith, we may feel that our expression of grief betrays our lack of faith. Belief in immortality does not necessarily guarantee that we can control our grief and sublimate our sorrow. We who have faith in life everlasting are not being untrue to our faith when we permit our real feelings of loss to find expression. Faith in life everlasting does not deny in any way the deep sense of loss we suffer when we lose a loved one. No religion denies that separation is painful. To mourn is legitimate and consistent with the Christian faith as long as we do not mourn excessively and hopelessly as those "who have no hope." The Christian religion justifies mourning. Our expression of grief is no indication of our lack of faith. Even our Lord wept at the tomb of His good friend Lazarus. Our religion should not be looked upon as a substitute for grief or as an instrument to suppress it. Instead, our religion gives us the power and strength to meet grief head-on, to pass through it, to rise above it, and to be strengthened by it.

Faith is not a means of short-circuiting grief; faith has the power to take our sorrow and transmute it into character and achievement. This is the very essence of the Christian faith. Our faith provides us the power by which we may be able to transform all experiences — whether good, bad, or indifferent — into the precious metal of Christ-like character. Faith is a divine alchemy that makes these elements yield a depth of maturity and Christ-likeness. Faith makes all things — good and bad —

work together for the spiritual good of all who love God. "We know that in everything God works for good with those who love him, who are called according to his purpose" (Rom. 8:28). Our religion teaches us how to bear sorrow, and in it we find the strength that will enable us to endure it in a worthy manner.

Almost all religions offer well-developed sacramental techniques to help us meet the challenge and advent of death and to veil the end of life with a halo of sacred solemnity. Maybe this is the reason why the older minister's manuals refer to the funeral as a "holy celebration." In addition to serving as expressions of faith, the rituals of religion for the dead provide us with the opportunity for a healthy, cleansing release of emotions. Through dogma, ritual, and sincere personal interest, our religion helps us to accept the pain of loss, maintain our contact with the living, and overcome our morbid guilt feelings through the medium of divine grace. In a very real and effective way, our religion performs its most heroic feat as we stand beside the grave.

We may not come to the true understanding of Christ's words, "Blessed are they that mourn for they shall be comforted," until we ourselves have actually mourned. Not until we are faced with the reality of loss, can we fully accept His comfort, feel His presence and help, and know that He holds our hand.

There are times when we might feel that in taking our loved one away God is punishing us. The idea that tragedy, sorrow, and suffering are the result of and the price for sin comes from the pronouncements of some whose experiences are recorded in the Old Testament of our Bible. Our New Testament is not in accord with such precepts. On several occasions Jesus corrected those who questioned Him regarding retribution. Luke 13:1-5 records the following incident: "There were present at that season some that told him of the Galileans, whose blood

Pilate had mingled with their sacrifices [apparently they were innocent victims]; and Jesus answering said unto them, Suppose ye that these Galileans were sinners above all the Galileans, because they suffered these things? I tell you, No. Or those eighteen upon whom the tower of Siloam fell, and slew them, think ye that they were sinners above all men that dwelt in Jerusalem? I tell you, No!" John 9:2-3 relates a similar response of our Lord when the disciples noticed a man blind from birth: "and his disciples asked him saying, Master, who did sin, this man, or his parents, that he was born blind? Jesus answered, Neither hath this man sinned, nor his parents."

The Bible can be a source of great strength and comfort to us in the time of sorrow. There are many passages that express the feelings and the faith of others who have also passed through the valley of weeping. A careful reading and study of these verses will enable us to make firmer the foundation of our faith in the ongoing purposes of God in our own lives and in the lives of our loved ones who have preceded us. We can find most helpful the following passages in the Old Testament: Deuteronomy 33:27; Joshua 1:9; II Samuel 12:18-23; Psalm 23; 27:1-10; 42:1-4; 46; 91; 121; Isaiah 25:8-9; 26:3; 40:28-31; 43:2. In the New Testament we can turn to Matthew 5:4; 11:28; John 11:25-26; 14:1-11, 18-21; 16:33; Romans 5:1-5; 8:38-39; 14:7-8; I Corinthians 15:20-28, 35-50, 53-58; II Corinthians 1:3-5; 4:13-14, 16-18; 5:1-8; Philippians 4:13; I Thessalonians 4:13-14; II Timothy 1:8-10; Revelation 21: 1-7.

As we read the Bible passages that refer to death, we become aware of the fact that the writers did not always call it death. They used expressions alive with beautiful meanings. The Psalmist spoke of passing "through the valley of the shadow of death that I might dwell in the house of the Lord"; Jesus spoke of dying as entering the Father's house of many mansions; Paul referred to death as putting off this tabernacle (tent) of clay that he might be clothed upon with an "eternal" garment; Peter spoke of death as an "entrance ministered abundantly," a great open door at the top of the roadway of life, etc. Why did they speak of death with words like these? We frequently employ figures of speech and euphemisms to lessen the emotional shock of the real meaning of a word or the experience it describes. In other words, we are afraid of it. The Biblical writers used euphemistic expressions for a very different reason — they were not afraid of death. They saw the other side of the phenomenon, for they possessed the instrument of faith which enabled them to understand death. Their experiences were much like ours as we look at ordinary sunlight through a glass prism. To our physical eye, unaided, sunlight appears plain, colorless, and ordinary, but when we view it through a prism, it reveals all the colors of the rainbow because sunlight is a composite of all the rainbow colors. Just as the prism helps our physical eye distinguish the radiant band of colors, so does the instrument of faith help us to understand death and bereavement.

As a people whose religious faith rests on the resurrection of Jesus Christ, we profess to believe in the resurrection and life everlasting. This doctrine teaches us that death is not the end but is only a transition to another room in our Father's house. Our loved ones are not lost; rather, they have only gone before us. For them the experience is one of gain rather than of loss. They have been loosed and freed from the limitations of the flesh. They are "absent from the body and present with the Lord" (II Cor. 5:8).

We may be tempted to dwell so long upon our own sense of loss that we completely lose sight of the experience of the one who has died. George MacDonald in *The Hidden Life* calls our attention to the fact that "death has two sides to it — one sunny and one dark, as this round world of ours is every day half sunny and half dark. We on the dark side call the mystery death; while they on the other, looking down in glad light await the glad birth with other tears than ours." Our Christian faith makes death "glorious and triumphant — for through its portals we enter into the presence of the living God."

The following story of "The Ship" has appeared in so very many versions and over so very many different names that today no one is really sure who wrote it the first time. It illustrates well the matter we are concerned with.

> I am standing on the seashore. A ship at my side spreads her white sails to the morning breeze and starts for the blue ocean. She is an object of beauty and strength, and I stand and watch her until she is only a ribbon of white cloud just where the sea and sky come to mingle with each other. Then someone at my side says, "There, she's gone." "Gone where?" Gone from my sight, that is all. She is just as large in mast and hull and spar as she was when she left my side, and just as able to bear her load of living freight to the place of destination. Her diminished size is in me, not in her; and just at the moment when someone at my side says, "There, she's gone," there are other voices ready to take up the glad shout: "There — she comes." And that is dying.

Even though we may profess a faith in the verities of the Christian religion, we may not always succeed in allowing these beliefs to guide our lives and our actions. Once a woman who professed to be a Christian stood at the open grave of her husband. Suddenly she screamed with uncontrolled and thoughtless emotion and no one could comfort her. A woman who knew her turned away in disgust, muttering: "Poor soul; I thought she believed it." People do watch us. They can tell whether our faith is only slushy sentiment that will melt under the dripping of tears or whether our confidence in God is the sort that will weather any storm.

From the past comes the story of a church school

superintendent and his wife who, on Good Friday, had buried their two daughters who had died of diphtheria. Probably no one in their fellowship expected them to be at their customary posts at the church on Easter Sunday; but they were there. The superintendent led the hymns with choking voice and his wife taught her class despite her tears. Following the service a lad, walking home with his father, remarked, "Dad, they sure believe it, don't they?" "Believe what?" the father inquired. "Oh, all this about Easter and eternal life." The father answered, "Of course — all Christians believe that." The boy replied: "I know, but they don't believe it like that."

When we lose our loved ones, we may be tempted to ask, "Why?" This may lead to tragic bitterness of soul. The clenched-fist method of dealing with our sorrow will make us tense and rebellious so that the healing, peace-giving power of God will not be able to get through to us. We may never understand the reason why our loved one was taken from us, but the fact that God had a reason should comfort us and is better than if we were able to find a dozen reasons. We spoke earlier of God's perfect will and His permissive will. Many experiences may come to us, His children, which He permits but has not ordered. This is what we mean by God's permissive will. Although we recognize the dangers inherent in seeking the "Why" of death, we also need to remember that at no time in our lives do we ever come closer to our Lord than when we ask, "Why?" Let us not forget that from His cross on the afternoon that He died our Lord asked, "Father, why hast thou forsaken me?"

In the past, the word "submission" was often used by some churchmen when they referred to the sorrows of life. Perhaps this connotation was unfortunate, for submission suggests a picture of one bowed down and crushed like a slave beneath the whip of his master. Today, we have a more positive word — "acceptance." When we accept something we acknowledge its presence, and in so doing we find comfort and peace. Perhaps acceptance was in the mind of our Lord when He said in the presence of disappointment, "Even so, Father, for so it seemed good in thy sight" (Matt. 11:26). Here we have the key to the whole matter. If we are able to accept life's difficult experiences and to remain at peace in our minds, it may be that the greater part of the victory will already have been won.

In conclusion, may we suggest that we surrender ourselves and our sorrows to the healing hands of God. If we will, we shall discover that God will provide healing if we but give Him the opportunity — but we must give Him that chance. It would be easy for God to spare a life, but He performs a greater miracle when He changes our life attitude. When what seems to be a tragedy actually becomes a triumph, and when what is a farewell rite becomes a coronation, God has performed His great miracle of spiritual healing. We should thank Him for the experience even though we do not understand.

We may never come to the place in our lives when the sense of bereavement will completely cease to be. God does not so promise. He promises us joy for the morning, and the Scriptures assure us that only in the great beyond will God wipe *all* our tears away. As long as mortal life lasts, we can avail ourselves of the comforting ministry of God through His Spirit. In Him there is grace to bind up our wounds and to heal our broken hearts. He will provide strength to undergird us lest we plunge into the abyss of despair. From Him comes the power that enables us to get back bravely into the stream of normal life again and assume our obligations with new vigor and resolve. "This is the victory that overcomes the world — even our faith" (I John 5:4).

Come, Ye Disconsolate

Come, ye disconsolate,
　　Where'er ye languish;
Come to the mercy seat,
　　Fervently kneel;
Here bring your wounded hearts,
　　Here tell your anguish;
Earth has no sorrow
　　That heaven cannot heal.

Joy of the desolate,
　　Light of the straying,
Hope of the penitent,
　　Fadeless and pure.
Here speaks the Comforter,
　　Tenderly saying,
"Earth has no sorrow
　　That heaven cannot cure."

Here see the bread of life,
　　See waters flowing
Forth from the throne of God,
　　Pure from above;
Come to the feast of life;
　　Come, ever knowing,
Earth has no sorrow
　　But heaven can remove.

Thomas Moore

By the Sea of Crystal

By the sea of crystal,
    Saints in glory stand,
Myriads in number,
    Drawn from every land.
Robed in white apparel,
    Washed in Jesus' blood,
They now reign in heaven
    With the Lamb of God.

Out of tribulation,
    Death and Satan's hand,
They have been translated
    At the Lord's command.
In their hands they're holding
    Palms of victory;
Hark! the jubilant chorus
    Shouts triumphantly:

"Unto God Almighty,
    Sitting on the throne,
And the Lamb, victorious,
    Be the praise alone.
God has wrought salvation,
    He did wondrous things;
Who shall not extol Thee,
    Holy King of Kings?"

William Kuipers

Jerusalem the Golden

Jerusalem the golden,
  With milk and honey blest,
Beneath thy contemplation
  Sink heart and voice oppressed.
I know not, O I know not
  What joys await us there,
What radiancy of glory,
  What bliss beyond compare!

They stand, those halls of Zion,
  All jubilant with song
And bright with many an angel
  And all the martyr throng.
The Prince is ever in them,
  The daylight is serene;
The pastures of the blessed
  Are decked in glorious sheen.

There is the throne of David;
  And there, from care released,
The song of them that triumph,
  The shout of them that feast;
And they who with their Leader
  Have conquered in the fight,
Forever and forever
  Are clad in robes of white.

Bernard of Cluny, Twelfth Century